THE ANCIENT WORLD

GREECE

Robert Hull

WAYLAND

THE ANCIENT WORLD

THE AZTECS · BENIN AND OTHER AFRICAN KINGDOMS EGYPT · GREECE · THE INCAS · ROME

Produced for Wayland Publishers Limited by
Roger Coote Publishing
Gissing's Farm, Fressingfield, Eye
Suffolk IP21 5SH, England

Editor: Alex Edmonds
Series editor: Alex Woolf
Designer: Victoria Webb
Map artwork: Peter Bull

First published in 1997 by
Wayland Publishers Limited, 61 Western Road
Hove, East Sussex BN3 1JD, England

Find Wayland on the Internet at http://www.wayland.co.uk

Cover pictures: A Greek soldier wearing a Corinthian helmet and carrying a shield (left), and an Olympic champion being crowned with his victory wreath.

British Library Cataloguing in Publication Data
Hull, Robert
    Greece. – (The ancient world)
    1.Greece – History – To 146 BC – Juvenile literature
    I.Title
    938

ISBN 07502 2054 6

Printed and bound in Italy by G. Canale & C.S.p.A., Turin

Picture acknowledgements: Ronald Sheridan, Ancient Art and Architecture Collection Ltd 4 (G.T. Garvey), 6, 8, 9, 10, 11, 18–19 (top), 20, 21 (Mike Andrews), 23, 25 (bottom), 27, 32, 39, 40–41, 44–45 (top), 46, 48–49 (bottom), 50, 51, 52–53 (bottom), 53 (top), 54, 56–57, 60; A. K. G Photo, London 5 (Erich Lessing), 30 (Erich Lessing), 37 (Erich Lessing), 38 (Erich Lessing), 43 (Erich Lessing), 44–45 (John Hios), 47 (Erich Lessing); British Museum 34–35; C. M. Dixon 13, 15, 16, 26, 29, 34 (British Museum), 36, 55, 58 (top), 58 (middle); E.T. Archive 19 (bottom); Michael Holford front cover (both), 28; Werner Forman Archive 24–25, 48.

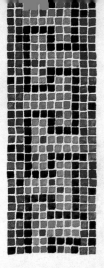

Contents

CHAPTER I

The Importance of Ancient Greece

The ancient civilization of Greece has been studied and admired ever since the Romans invaded Greece. As they absorbed Greece into their empire, they were impressed by its achievements. For centuries after this civilization had dissolved, Greek building techniques were copied, their texts were studied and their artists and sculptors were looked to for inspiration. Greek ideas on medicine, astronomy and geography were accepted without question, until as late as the seventeenth century.

Although it is 3,000 years old, ancient Greek civilization lives on in many areas of our lives. Music, philosophy, poetry, drama, politics – all of these disciplines come from Greek words and were pioneered in Greece. How this fascinating civilization came to create so much that we still use and enjoy is the greatest mystery about the ancient Greeks.

▼ Because so many Greeks live on islands they are great seafarers. For mainlanders too, in ancient times, it was often easier to sail along the coast than to travel over the rough and mountainous land. This is a typical Greek landscape, with the Aegean sea encircling the land.

The Geography of Ancient Greece

Greece is a land of towering mountains, encircled by sea and dozens of islands. Only about one fifth of Greek land is suitable for growing crops. However, the first farmers, like those of the late Stone Age people before them, also had

wild animals to hunt, fish to catch, fruits to pick and other plants and herbs to eat.

It was the land's riches that helped to make the civilized life of the ancient Greeks possible. In such a kind climate, life was lived mainly outdoors and homes were simple mud-brick houses. Greeks ate what their land provided for them: goat's cheese, honey, eggs, vegetables, fish, olives, figs and wine. The simplicity of their life, and the fact that many Greeks had slaves, gave Greeks time to talk, argue, vote, think, observe, socialize, invent, compose, write and sculpt.

Because the geography of the country made travel difficult, Greeks had to be completely self-sufficient. As a result, the Greeks became aware of their own responsibilities and developed a strong sense of their own worth. This characteristic gradually turned into the 'ideal' that runs throughout Greek religion, politics, philosophy and art; that as a Greek you should always be true to yourself and your state.

▼ The ruins of the Acropolis in Athens are a constant reminder of the achievements of ancient Greece. We know a lot about this civilization, from writings of the time, as well as from objects and buildings that have been dug up.

CHAPTER 2

The Early History

▼ Most Minoans made their living from farming, but hunting and fishing provided extra food for them. This fresco shows a young fisherman returning with his catch. We can also see from frescoes of Minoan ships, that they were a great trading and seafaring nation. The historian Thucydides also tells us about the legend of king Minos, which explains that he controlled a large and powerful fleet of ships.

The Greeks and Crete

The first people lived in Greece about 40,000 years ago. They were cave-dwellers and hunters. As early as 7000 or 8000 BC, the Greeks were travelling, trading and settling across the Aegean seas. Around 6000 BC farming was introduced to Greece. By 3000 BC, the Bronze Age, metal-workers were making bronze tools and weapons in Crete. From about 2200 BC, as the civilization flourished in Crete, writing, art and religion developed. The island was quite heavily populated with villages, towns and palaces. The most famous of these palaces now is Knossos, excavated in AD 1894 by Sir Arthur Evans. He called the non-Greek speaking people who lived on Crete during the Bronze Age, Minoan.

Minoan Knossos

The centre of the Minoan world was Knossos. The royal palace was as big as two football pitches and five storeys high. There were probably 10,000 people living in the house and grounds of the palace.

▶ This map shows the major Mycenaean settlements around Greece. Large settlements are marked by a circle and smaller ones are marked by squares. Important palaces are indicated by a diamond shape. The map also shows where Linear B tablets have been found.

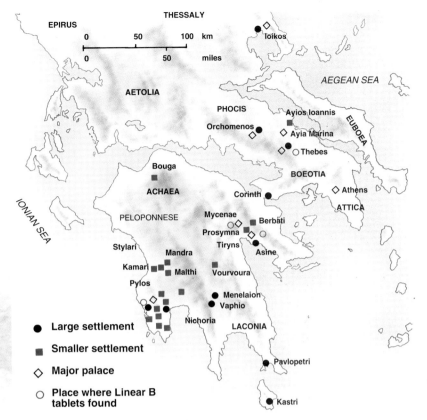

- ● Large settlement
- ■ Smaller settlement
- ◇ Major palace
- ○ Place where Linear B tablets found

What we know of Minoan life, dress and customs comes from wall paintings, called frescoes, pottery and other decorative objects discovered by archaeologists. In some Minoan frescoes we see young men and women performing a death-defying stunt – a running handstand over the back of a bull. Perhaps it was part of the religious worship of the bull, since this animal was sacred to the Minoans. Images of its horns were found across Knossos on pots, vases and tomb decorations.

Knossos was a very sophisticated palace. There were bright and colourful frescoes on the walls, and the royal apartments had sophisticated plumbing facilities: toilets were built over drains to carry away waste, and pipes brought in fresh water. By 2000 BC the Minoans had developed a hieroglyphic (picture) form of writing to help them keep good records. In 1900 BC they introduced a second script, Linear A; neither of these scripts has been translated yet.

Minoan meets Mycenaean

Around 1450 BC all of the palaces on Crete were destroyed, possibly this was caused by a volcano erupting on the island of Thera, nearby. Then the Mycenaeans, having invaded large areas of the mainland, arrived on Crete around 1450 BC; after this date there are signs that they lived in Knossos, and that the great palace was repaired and rebuilt.

Mycenae and Troy

Heinrich Schliemann was a German archaeologist. He believed that the *Iliad*, an eighth-century epic poem written by Homer about the siege of the city of Troy, was true. The poem tells how a force of Greeks sailed to Troy, in Asia Minor, to revenge the kidnapping of Helen, wife of the Spartan king. The expedition was led by King Agamemnon of Mycenae. The Greeks besieged Troy for ten years, then burned it down and sailed home. In AD 1870, at Hissarlik in modern Turkey, Schliemann found Troy, or rather several Troys, on top of each other like the storeys of a collapsed block of flats. He found ruined walls, fire-blackened stones and treasure: silver and gold vases, rings, knives and armour.

Using Homer's *Iliad* as a guide as to where to look, Schliemann then dug at the ruins of Mycenae, King Agamemnon's kingdom on mainland Greece, and uncovered royal graves, in deep shafts, dating from about 1600 to 1500 BC. The finds were breathtaking, there were many gold objects: masks, diadems, vases, drinking cups and necklaces.

▲ The tombs of the Mycenaean royal family were very elaborate. This tells us that the Mycenaeans probably believed in life after death. They buried their dead with wonderful treasures to be used in the afterlife. Historians can also tell that the Mycenaeans were a war-like people; armour and weapons found in graves, tell us that the Mycenaeans valued the qualities and skills of warriors.

At Knossos there was another strong hint that Homer's story of Greek chieftains sailing to Troy was true. Excavators found pottery showing shields of a kind mentioned in the Iliad: *they were in the shape of a figure eight, and were called 'tower shields'. Homer could never have seen one because by his time they were no longer used, yet he describes them perfectly. Perhaps the poets who first told Homer's stories saw them first-hand.*

Between about 1500 and 1200 BC, Mycenae was probably the strongest state in Greece and the centre of a trading and seafaring empire. During a fire at one of the Mycenaean palaces in 1200 BC, clay tablets containing household accounts were baked hard and preserved. In AD 1952, the script used to write these accounts, now called Linear B, was finally deciphered. It showed that the language of the tablets was Greek; the Mycenaeans had learned to write from the Minoans. Linear B used not only some signs from Linear A, but new signs which had been developed and added by the Mycenaeans.

By 1100 BC, the Mycenaeans had left the palace of Knossos. Other Mycenaean palaces of mainland Greece were also beginning to fall into ruins. This was the beginning of what we call the Dark Age, which lasted three hundred years, from 1100 to 800 BC. There was no writing during this time, so no records exist to tell us about this period. What we do know is that about this time the Greek-speaking Dorians became dominant in Greece.

▼ The wealth of the Mycenaeans is shown by the thin gold mask which Schliemann thought had belonged to Agamemnon himself. When Mycenaean kings died, their faces were usually covered with death masks of gold like this. Mycenaean civilization was rich in treasures; historians have even found thin sheets of gold that had been used as funeral wrappings for the bodies of two royal children.

CHAPTER 3

Out of the Dark Age

The End of the Dark Age

The Greek world gradually reawoke from the Dark Age. As the population started to increase again, after the collapse of the Mycenaean world, there was a major migration to the Ionian islands and to what is now Turkey. Then, in the eighth century BC there was a period of social, economic and cultural change. There were signs of recovery, such as a revival in the use of iron. As prosperity grew, and new towns were built, more pottery was produced and exported. Improvements in seafaring skills meant that Greeks in Euboea could set up trading posts in Syria, at Al Mina, and in the bay of Naples, in Italy.

Ancient Greek learning really progressed in the late to middle of the eighth century BC. Writing was rediscovered, this time using a true alphabet (from alpha and beta, its first two letters). The Greeks originally borrowed the idea from the Phoenicians, but created their own signs for the vowels. This new writing meant that accounts could be kept again and laws were recorded. This was also the time of the foundation of the Olympic Games, in 776 BC, in honour of the god Zeus.

▲ Inscribed onto this tablet is an example of the Phoenician script, which was adapted into the Greek alphabet. The earliest surviving piece of alphabetic writing comes from about 800 BC. By the middle of the eighth century BC, there are examples of people scratching their names on pots, using the new Greek method of writing. At the end of the seventh century BC, laws were being inscribed on stone.

The epic poems the *Iliad* and the *Odyssey*, the first two great stories of Greece – and of Europe – reached their final form in the same period. Although Homer is 'said' to have written them, he probably collected the stories in his huge memory. They are probably assembled from shorter tales, that had been passed down from various singers over the centuries. In the Dark Age there was no writing, so this was the only way to preserve the stories and legends of the past.

In other parts of Greece, more walled cities were built, which gradually developed into large, organized communities. These communities were formed as more land was cultivated and the population grew.

▶ Homer was the most famous poet in ancient Greece. He is often portrayed as having been blind. Men such as Homer were travelling poets who would learn stories of heroes, gods and goddesses and recite them to people. In the Dark Age there was no writing, so this was the only way to preserve the legends of the past. One tradition says that Homer was born near present-day Smyrna, in Turkey. Excavations have uncovered a walled city there, where Greeks settled in about 1000 BC. Homer describes such a developing city-state in the epic poem, the *Odyssey* :
'Around our city is a high fortified wall. There is a fine harbour on each side of the city, with a narrow entrance. Ships are drawn up on either side, and every man has a slipway. They assemble by the fine temple of Poseidon, with heavy paving sunk in the earth.'

Expanding Greece

In the eighth century BC, Greeks started to emigrate and set up new communities, often taking with them some 'sacred fire' from the mother-city, or *metropolis*. This 'fire' was probably ashes from the Delphic oracle. They would have used these to start their first sacrificial fire in their new home. They could ask for help from the *metropolis*, or even accept its officials, but the new communities were independent of the mother-city. When looking for areas to settle in, people looked for places with good trading opportunities. They also preferred areas that were not heavily populated, and did not have very developed political or social structures. This allowed them to put their own laws and systems in place.

New settlements shared a common culture with the Greek homeland. When Athens attacked and failed to defeat the colony at Syracuse in 413 BC, the victorious Syracusans gave aid and shelter to the Athenian prisoners, in return for readings of the plays of Euripides the tragedian.

▼ This map shows the main imports to Greece. It also shows the areas where Greeks established new settlements.

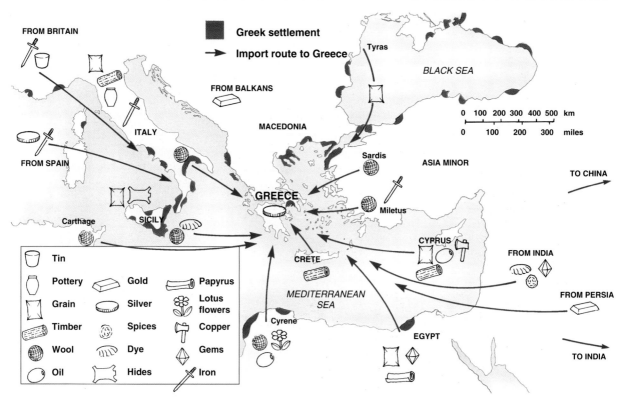

FROM BRITAIN

FROM BALKANS

FROM SPAIN

Greek settlement

Import route to Greece

Tyras

BLACK SEA

ITALY

MACEDONIA

0 100 200 300 400 500 km
0 100 200 300 miles

Sardis

ASIA MINOR

TO CHINA

GREECE

Miletus

Carthage

SICILY

CRETE

CYPRUS

FROM INDIA

MEDITERRANEAN SEA

FROM PERSIA

Cyrene

EGYPT

TO INDIA

Tin			
Pottery	Gold		Papyrus
Grain	Silver		Lotus flowers
Timber	Spices		Copper
Wool	Dye		Gems
Oil	Hides		Iron

Sicily was so successful with its colonies that it was later known to the Romans as Magna Graecia, 'Greater Greece'. Its main city, Syracuse, was bigger than any Greek city. There were new settlements like this all round the Mediterranean and beyond, as far as the northern shores of the Black Sea. Iron, gold, fish, wood and leather were all sent back to Greece.

In time, the 20 or 30 leading cities of Greece became hundreds of independent cities, scattered throughout the Mediterranean and beyond. The island of Miletus alone, had sent out and set up over 60 settlements. Many modern cities that are a very long way from Greece began as Greek settlements. We now know Massilia, Antipolis, Nicaea and Maenace, as Marseilles, Antibes, Nice and Monaco. Socrates summed up the Greeks' expanding culture, when he said that the Greeks lived round the Mediterranean 'like frogs round a pond'.

▲ The first coins were probably used at the end of the seventh century BC in Asia Minor. Gradually they spread to the Ionian colonies and then to mainland Greece. It was a sign of independence when a city issued its first coins. They were usually made in silver or gold. The image used on the coin was often the symbol of the city issuing the coin; perhaps an animal or a god or goddess, or a famous patron of the city. This coin comes from Macedonia and shows the god Dionysus on a mule, drinking wine.

Herodotus describes the Phocaeans from Ionia as being excellent sailors:
'These Phocaeans were the first of the Greeks to make long sea voyages, and they were the ones who discovered the Adriatic seas, Etruria, Iberia and Tartessos.'
The Phocaeans fled to Sicily and Corsica to escape Persian domination. They settled there, and became successful traders. This enraged the Phoenicians, who went to war with them over trading opportunities.

13

CHAPTER 4

The Birth of Democracy

The geography of Greece meant that towns more than a few kilometres from each other had little contact. There was not enough communication between them for them to work together, or link up politically. They therefore became individual 'states'. By the middle of the sixth century BC there were hundreds of separate states across the Greek world. Each of these was called a *polis*.

Greek states were small. On the island of Kea for example, which is only 130 km² in area, there were four independent states. In their mini-states the Greeks were competitive and individualistic. Despite the aggressive independence of these *poleis*, a very strong Greek culture grew up at this time. Individuals travelled great distances to make contact, and trade with other Greeks. Herodotus the Greek historian explains this feeling of Greekness:

'We are all Greek,' he wrote 'we have the same language, the same gods and temples and way of life.'

▲ This map shows the Greek city states of Attica. Early villages in Attica were walled, but as villages expanded, more of the settlements had walls built around them for defence. The harbours in Attica were important for developing trade.

14

◀ The picture from a vase shows a farm worker gathering saffron, a valuable spice, from crocus flowers. Before Solon, in Athens many farmers had to give up a sixth of their harvest to pay off debt. These farmers were called *hektemoroi*, meaning 'sixth-part men'. If they could not get out of debt they might be sold as slaves. By 600 BC many Athenian farmers were falling into debt and being made slaves.

Nobles and Tyrants

In Homer's stories, there are kings who ruled over the *poleis*. Later, it was aristocratic families who controlled them. From the sixth century BC, writers refer to ruling families of nobles, such as the Bacchiadae family who ruled over Corinth. Aristocrats, like the Bacchiadae, became powerful originally because they were the only people who could afford to buy the horses and armour necessary to take part in wars. So, because they had the equipment they became the leaders.

As an increase in trade brought wealth to more people, tradesmen and merchants began to demand a say in government. With their money, they could get enough support from fellow Greeks to take power from those who had it. So, from about 660 BC, across the Greek world many ruling families were thrown out of power, by *tyrannoi* or tyrants. These tyrants were ambitious men who overthrew the governments of the *polis*. Although the word 'tyrant' now describes someone who is harsh and unjust, in ancient Greece the name simply meant 'ruler'.

The Greek identity was so strong that during the Olympic Games, wars between states were somehow suspended. This was done to prevent offence to the gods, in whose honour the games were held. But, in 420 BC, during the Peloponnesian war, Sparta was banned from competing. The contests then had to take place under armed guard.

Solon and Peisistratus

In Athens, around 600 BC, there was a lot of dissatisfaction with the very strict debt laws. It would not have been surprising if a tyrant had taken advantage of Athens' problems and taken control of the *polis*. This did not happen though; in Athens in 594 BC, Solon, chief *archon* (holder of state office) took control. There were nine *archons* or magistrates, who were advised by the *areopagus* or Council, which consisted of former *archons*. The *areopagus* was a very important court in Athens in the sixth century BC. Once in power, Solon immediately cancelled the farmers' debts, so they could now work their land without fear of being enslaved. He also brought back out of slavery those who had been sold into it. These were the first steps towards building a democracy.

▼ Peisistratus encouraged an era of cultural achievements. Under him, Athens turned into a beautiful city. Later, the advances that had been made in architecture, under Peisistratus' rule, produced many fabulous buildings, like the temple of Olympian Zeus (*below*). This was the largest shrine in European Greece.

Athenian citizens were also involved in the running of the law-courts. Later, in the fifth century BC, Pericles introduced pay for attending them – it was two obols a day originally. One writer says a family of four, living carefully, might have managed on two and a half obols a day. Juries at the courts were chosen by lot. A full court for important cases needed 501 jurors, with less for smaller or private cases. Later, citizens were also paid for attending the Assembly.

Then Solon gave more power to poorer people. He set up a People's Court, where any citizen, however poor, could bring a prosecution. He also divided Athenians into four classes. Every Athenian belonged to one group, depending on their wealth, calculated in terms of their annual production of corn, oil, and wine. He gave powers to each group, which meant that many who had had no influence or power before, in the running of the *polis*, now did. Solon explained why he had never become a tyrant when he said: 'Tyranny is a fine place to be, but there is no way down from it.'

After Solon, there was much political unrest and disagreement. Eventually, there was a tyranny in Athens, under Peisistratus, who had been a very successful soldier. He was a mild tyrant who had attempted to gain power many times before; once by going into Athens with a woman dressed as the goddess Athene, to prove that he had the support of the patron goddess of Athens! When he eventually took control, he began various public works schemes: improving the water supply and starting the construction of a new temple to Athene, as well as other buildings. He loaned farmers his own money and took land from his enemies to give to peasants.

Democracy

It was in 508 BC under Kleisthenes that full democracy was first introduced. He reorganized the constitution to make it a democracy, meaning 'rule by the people'. Although we now understand democracy as a system which allows everyone to vote, in Athens in the sixth century BC only citizens could vote. Citizenship was limited, three-quarters of the population of Athens were not citizens: those under 18, women, *metics* (foreign residents), temporary visitors and slaves. Only citizens could own property, go to all festivals and attend the Assembly.

Kleisthenes gave citizenship back to many who had lost it under the tyrants, so that now every free man was a citizen. He created ten tribes instead of four, organizing them so that they represented all Attica – town, country and coast. There was a new Council of 500 people, with 50 people from each tribe who were chosen by lot.

Now every male citizen was a member of the Assembly, or *ecclesia*. About 6,000 people seem to have attended regularly, out of about 30,000 to 40, 000 citizens, in a total population of about 250,000. The right to attend also meant the right to speak and vote.

▲ By the fifth century BC, laws were being inscribed in stone all across Greece. This inscription (*above*), from Gortyn in Crete, is about family and property law. It states that slaves could own property, and even marry free women in Crete. The first written laws in Athens had come just before Solon and were the cause of a lot of the discontent felt by Athenians. They were laid down by the magistrate Draco in 621–20 BC and were very harsh. One law said that you could be put to death for stealing a cabbage.

A rope, dripping with red paint, hauled in the people who were slow to volunteer, branding them as unpatriotic. A vote in the Assembly, by a show of hands, decided important state matters, such as whether Athens should go to war, and how public money should be spent. The Assembly debated proposals which were put to them by the Council.

Kleisthenes also introduced ostracism, the ritual of voting to send someone into exile. If an official was corrupt, or a general failed in his duties, they could be voted into exile. Ostraca were bits of broken pottery, on which the names of those proposed for ostracism were scratched. Every member of the Assembly wrote the name of the official that he wished to see ostracised on the piece of pottery. If there were more than 6,000 votes against one person, he had to leave Athens for ten years.

▼ The Persians came from what is now Iran. In the sixth century BC they were expanding their lands. This frieze was in the palace of King Darius at Persepolis. It was under Darius that the Persian Empire grew to its largest.

The Persian Threat

Early on in the fifth century BC, the strength of Greek civilization was about to be tested by one of the biggest empires in the world – the Persian Empire.

First the Persians took over Lydia and its Greek Ionian cities. Then, in 499 BC, with the help of Athens and Eretria, the Greek Ionians rebelled. The Persians immediately reconquered them, leaving the Greeks in no doubt about the power of the Persian empire.

King Darius gathered 100,000 troops and nearly 500 ships, and conquered the Aegean islands. Then in 490 BC, the Persians landed at Marathon in Attica. They would not easily forgive Athens for having helped the Ionian cities. Athens sent for help to Sparta, but the Spartans could not come because they were celebrating a festival. The Athenians had to fight the Persians alone. When the Spartans eventually arrived, they were horrified at the number of Athenians that lay dead on the battlefield. But, the Athenians had beaten the Persians against all the odds. At that battle, at Marathon, 6,400 Persians were killed and only 192 Athenians, according to Herodotus. One reason for the Greeks' superiority was their way of fighting, using the *phalanx*. In this formation, infantry soldiers carrying shields and long spears walked forward in densely packed order. When the first rank fell the second took over, and so on.

Ten years later, in 480 BC, the second Persian invasion took place under Darius' son Xerxes. This time the Greeks lost a crucial land battle at a narrow mountain pass, called Thermopylae. The Persians had been shown a way round the back of the mountain by a treacherous Greek farmer.

The Persians had more soldiers than the Greeks. Greek hoplite armour included a long spear, bronze helmet and leg-guards, and a heavy wooden shield with a bronze rim. The Persians had spears, bows and wicker shields. Their heads were only covered with cloth.

► The *trireme* was the main warship, on both sides, in the Persian wars. It voyaged under sail, then the 170 oarsmen drove it into battle. There were only a few soldiers on board, because the idea was to disable enemy ships with the metal-tipped ram. This picture shows a life-size replica of a *trireme*.

The Battle of Salamis

Xerxes marched on into Attica, to attack Athens. Many Athenians were so scared that they wanted to retreat to the Peloponnese. They moved on instead, to the island of Salamis, leaving the Persians to burn down Athens. The Athenians and the other Greeks took their ships into the narrow bay at Salamis. There, the Athenian general Themistocles arranged for the Persians to be given a false tip-off; he saw to it that they were told that the Greeks were about to leave. The larger Persian fleet moved in to trap the Greek ships, but there wasn't enough space for the Persian fleet to manoeuvre. Large numbers of Persian ships were rammed, and many others just lurched into each other. This was a major defeat for the Persians.

The real end of the Persian invasion was marked at the battle of Plataea in 479 BC. The Greeks put together a large army, led by the Spartan general Pausanias. In this surprise victory, 100,000 Persians fought and lost against only 40,000 Greeks. Whilst the Greek army was defeating the Persians on land, the Greek navy was attacking and burning the Persian fleet at Mykale, in Asia Minor. The Persian threat had been repulsed at last.

Simonides, a friend of the Athenian general Themistocles, wrote several epitaphs for men who had died in battles against the Persians. This one, composed in honour of the Spartans who died at the battle of Thermopylae, became famous: 'We obeyed orders. Here we lie. Tell them in Sparta, passer-by.'

CHAPTER 5

Athens, Sparta and Fifth-Century Greece

The Delian League

The Persians had been turned back by Athenian naval power, and the support given to Athens by other Greek *poleis*. There was, however, a fear that the Persians might try to invade Greek states again. Now, in fear of the Persians, other *poleis* voluntarily joined Athens in what was called the Delian League. This name is used because it was created in 477 BC at a meeting on the island of Delos, sacred to Apollo. Until 454 BC the league had its treasury on the island.

This league of allied states, led by Athens, wanted to make sure that the Persians didn't threaten them, or other Greek territories. Although the Persians had been prevented from invading mainland Greece, they still had disagreements with the Greeks. They fought with them over territories around the Mediterranean, in places like Cyprus and Egypt. Wars against Persia continued until 449 BC and the 'Peace of Callias'.

The Golden Age

By the middle of the fifth century BC, the Delian League had become an Athenian empire. When some states found it easier to contribute cash rather than ships, Athens collected and looked after this tribute money, called *phoros*. Reluctant allies who wanted to leave the alliance were forced back in by Athens. After 454 BC the treasury was transferred to Athens. Athens was now growing in power.

▶ Although Pericles was passionately interested in rebuilding and beautifying Athens, there was another side to his building programme. At a time when Athens had to recover economically from its war with Persia, the building of these huge monuments was a great way of showing off the power and prosperity of Athens. One such building project was the Parthenon. This picture shows how the Parthenon would have looked in the fifth century BC. Inside is the cult statue of Athena. It was made of gold and ivory and was 12 m high.

In 454 BC, the enormous sum of 8,000 talents, from the Delian League, was being housed in the Parthenon. Its back room had become the treasury. For comparison, a **trireme** cost three talents, and the great building programme of Pericles' time, including the Parthenon and other buildings on the Acropolis, cost over 2,000 talents. Pericles told people that as head of the League, Athens deserved some rewards for the military and administration duties that it undertook. This is how he justified spending money from the Delian League on Athens.

Athens' position at the head of the League gave it enormous power. But, just as Athens dominated progress in Greece, Pericles dominated Athens. Pericles was a very powerful politician, a *strategos*, or military leader. He was respected for being a very persuasive speaker and for supervising the rebuilding of Athens after it was sacked by the Persians. Pericles also encouraged every citizen to take part in the day to day running of the legal system. This period is often called the Golden Age. It was a time when trade brought great wealth to Athens, the arts flourished and people flocked to live and study there. During this period, Athens was the cultural centre of Greece.

▼ The Acropolis was the military and religious centre of Athens. It contained many temples and shrines, like the Temple of Athena Nike, shown below. When they entered Athens in 480 BC the Persians destroyed many buildings in Athens, including temples and shrines. This temple was built after the Persian invasion.

The Legal System

There were no lawyers, judges or officials in Greece: citizens had to undertake their own legal cases. Jurors at court were given two bronze ballot tokens to vote with. When the trial finished, the juror would have to hand in one of the tokens to indicate whether he felt that the person on trial was innocent or guilty. One of the tokens was solid, which meant innocent, the other had a hollow middle and meant guilty.

The writer Plutarch describes how an Athenian politician and his supporters denounced Pericles for squandering money:
'Greece must be outraged… and consider this an act of blatant tyranny, when she sees that with the contribution she has been compelled to make towards the war we are gilding and beautifying our city, like some vain woman decking herself in precious jewels.'

▼ Any citizen could serve on the jury, all he had to do was turn up at the court. In the fourth century BC, this device, called a *kleroteria*, was used to pick a jury by lot. Coloured balls were dropped into the machine and they fell at random next to the names of all the volunteers. The colour of ball next to your name decided whether you served that day or not.

▼ A form of slavery is mentioned in Linear B tablets found in Mycenae. They date back in Greek history as far as the Bronze Age. Slavery in Athens only became important in the sixth century BC. Despite the fact that it was an accepted part of everyday life, the tragedian Euripides bravely spoke out against it, calling it: 'That thing of evil, forcing submission from man to what no man should yield to.' Made in a Greek city in southern Italy around the first century BC, this terracotta vessel shows a comic impersonating a slave, who is sitting on an altar.

Slaves and Metics

In the fourth and fifth centuries BC slaves formed a large part of the population. There might have been between 60,000 and 150,000 slaves in Athens at this time. Even some fairly poor families seemed to have had a slave helper. Slaves were either born into slavery from slave parents or they became slaves. You could become a slave by being captured in war, or kidnapped, perhaps by pirates. Sometimes even your own people would sell you into slavery.

Slaves were often hired out by their owners to work the mines, or were required to carry equipment and baggage to war. They fought for their cities, but only in times of great crisis, as they did for Athens against the Spartans. As a reward for this loyalty, they might then be given their freedom.

In some Greek cities there was a large group of resident foreigners, non-citizens called metics. These immigrants were often traders and craftsmen, or artists and philosophers from other cities. In Athens there were perhaps 25,000 metics. They paid taxes, owned slaves and had the right to attend some festivals, though not to vote in the Assembly. They could not own land or houses either.

◀ Slaves were employed in just about every work activity in Greece, whether it was skilled or unskilled. The two biggest areas that slaves were employed in were household duties and mining. Agriculture also needed a lot of slave labour. The picture on this vase shows farmworkers picking olives. In his book, the *Oeconomicus*, the writer Xenophon tells us that most gentlemen farmers lived in the city. They left the running of their estates to slave workmen and a slave bailiff. Slaves lives were often very hard; Aristotle described a slave's life as 'work, punishment and food'.

The writer Xenophon complained about the way that slaves and metics mixed easily in Athens with citizens, 'Slaves and metics are allowed great freedom in Athens. You are not allowed to hit them, and a slave will not stand to one side to let you pass… Even if there were a law to say that a slave or metic could be struck by a free man, you might hit a free Athenian thinking he was a slave, because the people are no better dressed than slaves or metics…'

Athens and Sparta

Democracy was not an Athenian invention. Plenty of other Greek *poleis* had councils and assemblies. Many of these states did not have enough people to supply the thousands of citizens who were needed to vote in the Athenian Assemblies. In other states, citizenship was confined to a small number of well-off people, an *oligarchy,* meaning 'rule by a few'. At various times, even Athens itself had been an *oligarchy.*

In the fifth century BC, the strongest *oligarchy* was Sparta. Sparta was unique because its freedom depended on the population of a conquered state, Messenia, whose people all became *helots. Helots* were half way between being free and being slaves. They could own property, but otherwise they were enslaved to the Spartans. One poet said that they were treated 'just like donkeys'. The citizens of Sparta depended on allies for their army; many of them fought at Plataea against the Persians. There were always many more *helots* than Spartans, so arming them was dangerous, and Sparta was so nervous that the *helots* might rebel that wars far from home were avoided if possible. There were several *helot* uprisings.

▲ This statue shows a Spartan woman athlete. Spartan women seemed very free and undignified to other Greeks. To make them strong and healthy for child-bearing, they were expected to enter athletic competitions. During these competitions they wore what other Greeks saw as shockingly short tunics. Spartan girls even exercised naked, as did the boys and men.

Part of the Spartans' training for their young men was a ritual called the krypteia. *According to Plutarch, young men 'at night would go through the fields and do away with the most powerful and sturdiest helots'. This was not counted as murder, but war. Aristotle says that the Spartan* ephors, *or leading officials, 'would declare war on the helots, so that killing them did not involve ritual pollution.'*

Spartan Training

Sparta was obsessed with war, and brought up its young men to be tough soldiers. From the age of seven, they lived away from home, boarding in barracks-like schools. They went barefoot, had only one cloak a year and just enough to eat. Spartans lived a military-style life, rather than a family life. There was even family spying; wives could bring charges of disloyalty to Sparta against their husbands. Spartan courage, however, was famous. One Spartan, who was told at Thermopylae that the enemy numbers were so large that their arrows would hide the sun, said 'Fine, we shall be able to fight in the shade.' A Spartan poet said:

'He who falls in the front of the line and loses his life, brings honour to his city, his family and his father.'

In this tough world, cowards were outcasts, they could not marry or even eat in the public messes. So as to be recognized in the street, cowards had a cloak with coloured patches and partly shaved beards. Aristotle did not respect Spartan values. He once said that focusing on military success alone might lead to victories, but it doesn't give you the intelligence to know how to put them to good use.

▼ Pericles was known to have been a haughty and distant man, as well as very stubborn. It was even suggested that he had dragged the people of Athens into war against the Spartans, just to further his career. It was rumoured that he felt that he was losing power in politics and knew that the Athenians would need him in a time of war.

The Peloponnesian War

In the middle of the fifth century BC, Greece became divided into two groups of states. Athens was the centre of a growing naval empire. It was also the city of great dramatists, artists and visiting poets and singers. But Sparta, ever suspicious, was convinced that Athens was getting too powerful. It too had gathered its own league of allies, mostly from around the Peloponnese.

Between 431 BC and 404 BC there was a war between Athens and Sparta and their allies. Pericles was the Athenian leader at the start of the Peloponnesian war. Because Sparta had the stronger land army, Pericles' risky strategy was to withdraw the people of Attica into Athens, and let Sparta attack the surrounding land. Athens had constructed 'Long Walls' running down to the harbour, so she had regular supplies from overseas. However, the pressure of people in the city meant terrible overcrowding and brought on a plague in which Pericles died. Meanwhile, because Sparta had no Athenian army to fight, it was able to destroy Attica's villages and devastate its fields, vineyards and olive groves.

In the Peloponnesian war, Athens won some victories and Sparta won others. Sparta had a very powerful army, but their navy was not equal to that of Athens. Many times the Spartan army destroyed areas around Athens, but they never actually managed to get past the great walls of the city.

▲ Wars were seen as the ultimate test of a man. The Delphic frieze celebrates the war-like spirit of the Greeks. To die in battle was a real honour. This was denied to many of the Greek soldiers during the Peloponnesian war. A terrible plague struck Athens and killed many of them, before they even got to war. The historian Thucydides had estimated how many died in the army. He wrote that 4,400 cavalry died out of 26,000. Tragically, 4,000 men died in a camp before the battle of Poteidaia, 1,050 of them in just 40 days.

In the last few years of the war Sparta was helped by Persian money. In 415 BC, an Athenian expedition sailed to conquer Sicily. Alcibiades, one of its senior commanders, fled to the Spartans because he had a trial to face back in Athens. In 413 BC the Athenian forces were completely wiped out. Nearly 200 triremes and 30,000 men were lost. It was a crushing defeat.

To make matters worse, Athens lost a lot of its population through plague between 430 and 426 BC. There were also revolts by some Athenian subjects, as well as periods of undemocratic rule by *oligarchs* in Athens itself. In 411 BC there was a period of violent rule by a council of 400 men, who temporarily abolished democracy.

Finally, the Spartans built their own fleet and won an important sea battle in 405 BC, in the Hellespont. The Spartans captured 170 out of 180 Athenian ships. With the Hellespont under Spartan control, the Athenian navy could not protect the ships bringing grain from the lands around the Black Sea. In 404 BC, after a long, hard winter under siege, Athens was starving and was forced to surrender to Sparta. Despite Spartan supremacy, democracy was restored to the Athenian government in 403 BC. For the next 50 years there were many problems and disputes continuing between the various Greek states. These problems distracted the Greeks from the growing power of one particular Greek state, Macedonia, which lies in the north-east of Greece.

Pericles praised the Athenian constitution in a speech commemorating the soldiers killed early in the Peloponnesian war:
'We possess a constitution which does not imitate the laws of others, in fact we are an example to others. The constitution's name is democracy, because the majority manage its affairs, not just a few. Everybody is equal when private disputes are being settled… nobody is prevented by poverty from taking part in public life… we conduct our political life with freedom … we are unique in considering the man who takes no part in the affairs of the city not as one who minds his own business but as one who is totally useless'.

CHAPTER 6

Living in Ancient Greece

At Home

The houses of ordinary Greeks were in great contrast to the large public buildings. Not many Greek houses have survived, but archaeologists have discovered the remains of some small, cramped dwellings. Some houses were built into the rocky hillside, with levelled floors and walls built up from the rock with mud bricks. Mud bricks were made by shaping and drying mud. The walls of houses were therefore not as hard as those of modern brick. They could easily be tunnelled through by burglars, but were probably safer than brick during an earthquake because of their flexibility. These walls had small window-openings with no glass in, and they often faced inwards onto a small courtyard. Bigger houses might have a fountain in the courtyard where a well provided water. Most homes would also have an altar in the courtyard where prayers were said.

Men and women often used separate rooms. The women would eat in their quarters, the *gynaeceum*, where they would carry out household duties and see their friends. The men used a different room in the house, called the *andron*, to eat meals and entertain friends.

▼ For women from poorer families, many of the daily household duties that were expected of them, allowed them to socialize with other women. The women painted on this vase are collecting water from a fountain. They would have been able to meet their friends and talk as they filled their jars.

Only on one or two occasions were Athenian women involved in legal transactions about property. One was when they were betrothed, and their guardian brought the dowry (the cash gift to the future husband). The ceremony did not involve the woman speaking, and went like this:

> *'I give this woman for the procreation of legitimate children.*
> *I accept.*
> *And two talents dowry (or whatever amount was offered).*
> *I agree.'*

Girls might marry as young as 14. Once they were married, they lost any freedom they would have had as a young girl. When husbands brought friends home for a meal, the wife would not join them. Most women from good families don't seem to have gone out much, except for occasions like funerals or weddings, or to shop for important items. Whenever they went out, they were accompanied by a slave.

Women and the Family

Greek life was based around the household, the *oikos*. The *oikos* included every aspect of the family, the male head of it plus other family members, and even the family slaves. Houses, property and land and the family tombs were also part of the *oikos*.

Athenian women couldn't own property or deal in important business. They were owned by a *kyrios*, the father, husband or close male relative. Their job was to take care of children, supervise servants, and look after the house itself. In other states, such as Sparta, women had more freedom and legal status.

In the Oeconomicus, *the Athenian writer Xenophon describes the wife's duties: 'to stay indoors and superintend the servants... to see to any servant who is sick... to keep an eye on the baking woman... to stand by the housekeeper when she is measuring out... to go round and see if everything is in its right place'. One very important duty was to 'stand before the loom like a mistress'.*

Women from poorer families had more freedom of a kind, simply because they did not have slaves to do all the household duties and had to go out and about themselves, shopping and water collecting. Some women, mainly from poorer classes, went out to sell flowers or bread in the market. Euripides' mother was supposed to have sold vegetables.

One group of Greek women who were unusually free to go about as they pleased, were the *hetairai*. These women were trained to become companions for men. They were usually quite well-educated and pretty. They would be invited to men's dinner parties to join in with the discussions, and to play music to the guests.

▼ These two girls are playing knucklebones, a game similar to dice, which involved throwing small animal bones in the air and catching them. Women would sometimes go to visit their friends, to talk and play games like knucklebones; but they did not have the freedom to socialize that men did.

Second-class Citizens

Women did not play a very active part in Greek society. They had no involvement in politics or law. The philosopher Aristotle said: 'The ability to think is not present in slaves. It does not work in women… the male is by nature superior.'

Some women did become famous or achieved positions of power. In sport, a Spartan woman called Kyniska owned horses and chariots that won the chariot race at the Olympic Games in 396 BC and 392 BC. Other Spartan women later achieved the same thing. Some women had positions of importance in Greek life. Pericles had a mistress, Aspasia, who was said to have helped him to write his speeches. She was also famous for turning her home into a centre of intellectual discussion and debate.

Growing Up and Going to School

Education had to be paid for in most city-states, and it was not usually for the poor, or for girls – except for a very few. Outside Sparta, girls usually stayed at home and learned household skills from their mothers. Schooling for boys had three elements. A *grammatistes* taught them reading, writing and arithmetic; a *kitharistes* taught music and poetry; and a *paidotribes* taught dancing and athletics.

Often the boy's education was overseen by a *paidogogus*, a slave who sat in on the child's classes and made sure he didn't misbehave.

At school, pupils wrote with a sharpened stick, on wooden tablets coated in wax. They learned about numbers using an abacus – a kind of counting frame with beads on wires – or just using pebbles.

▲ The philosopher Plato taught at a *gymnasium* like the one above. Boys stayed at school until they were about 15. Then they might voluntarily go to a *gymnasium*, a place where they could exercise; they could also listen to teachers of more difficult knowledge. It was at places like this that the great philosophers, such as Plato, taught in the fourth century BC.

In Sparta, babies were the soldiers, or mothers of soldiers, of the future. They therefore needed to be healthy. Officials decided whether each new-born baby was strong enough to live. If it was not, the baby was left on the hillside to die.

Greek Dress

Greek dress was simple. Both men and women wore a piece of cloth, called a *chiton,* around the body, pinning it at the shoulder. Men wore it to the knee, women to the ankle. It could be worn in various ways, but basically it was like a sack, with openings for the head and arms. Then there was the *himation*, a kind of cloak, which again both men and women wore; the *peplos*, an outer garment, was worn by women. People wore sandals or slippers, or soft boots reaching up the calf.

Leisure

Children of wealthy families played with dolls, hoops and sticks, and even yoyos. Younger Greek children had little two-wheeled carts to pull about. Vases and sculptures show us that older children bowled hoops or went fishing. Greek adults often played board games too.

▼ One activity that Greek men enjoyed very much was animal fighting. This involved getting two dogs, cockerels or other creatures to fight with each other, and betting on which one would win. The animals usually had to fight to the death.

Adults in Greece enjoyed many different sports and games. Sport was encouraged in Greece, since it kept the citizens fit, and ready if war broke out. Chariot racing and horse racing were very popular. Greek men boxed, wrestled and ran, in sporting events. The Greeks invented the *Pentathlon*, a competition involving five events: running, wrestling, jumping, discus and javelin.

Dinner parties were a popular social activity in the evening. After the food was finished, the guests would sit around drinking and talking or listening to music and reciting poetry. During the day, men often went to the *agora*, or market place. Here traders, politicians and craftsmen would meet and discuss business, or talk to friends. The *agora* was the business centre of the town, as well as the social centre.

CHAPTER 7

Gods and Religion

Religion was very important to the Greeks. Every activity in Greek life had a religious aspect to it. The Spartans would even be late for battles because they had been celebrating a religious ritual. Although Greek religion had no 'church' as such, there were common beliefs across the Greek world. These were often based on the Greek myths, the stories about the exploits of the Greek gods. In addition to this, there were local gods and cults which developed across the Greek world.

The Gods

Most of what the Greeks believed about their gods came from Homer's stories, and from Hesiod, whose *Theogony* is a story about the struggles of the gods. He tells us that the Olympians were a family of gods, who lived on Mount Olympus. The only two gods that didn't live there were Hades the King of the Underworld, and Dionysus the god of wine and celebration.

In Homer's stories the gods look human and behave like humans – gossiping, quarrelling and falling in love. They could be cruel, jealous and selfish, as well as kind and helpful. Unlike humans, they did not die. Some of the gods involved themselves in human lives and helped people. They sometimes even appeared to them to give them guidance, as Athene often does to Odysseus in Homer's *Odyssey*.

▲ According to legend, one day Zeus had a headache. To relieve it, he ordered Hephaestus to open his skull. As soon as it had been done, Athene jumped out of Zeus' head, in full armour. This vase shows a scene from the legend of the birth of Athene.

The Olympians

Zeus was leader of the gods. He was lord of the skies, the wind and thunder. His favourite weapon was the thunderbolt. Hera was his wife, and the goddess of marriage. Poseidon was Zeus' brother. He was also the god of the sea; he rode the waves, in a chariot drawn by horses that he had tamed. In pictures he is often seen carrying a trident, which he used to split open the earth, causing earthquakes. The Greeks believed that their fate on the seas lay in the hands of Poseidon.

One of Zeus' daughters was Athene, the war-like protector of Athens. She wore a goat skin, with a picture of a Gorgon's head, and live snakes dangling from it. It was Athene who brought the first olive to Athens, and invented spinning, weaving and other arts. The young and beautiful Apollo was god of music, healing and prophecy. His weapon was the bow and arrows. Artemis was his twin sister. She was goddess of the wild and hunting.

Hermes was the god of merchants, travellers and thieves. He was the messenger-god, and the most cunning of the Olympians. Awkward and lame, Hephaestus was the blacksmith-god. He was married to the beautiful Aphrodite, the goddess of love, beauty, marriage and fertility. Aphrodite was worshipped all over the world. Ares was god of war. He liked fighting, and blood and death. He was not a very popular god in Greece. Demeter was the goddess of corn and the harvest. It was Demeter who taught people how to plough and sow.

▲ As far back as the Mycenaean times, gods such as Zeus, Poseidon and Dionysus are mentioned in records, along with others that did not survive into Classical Greece. This bronze bust (*above*) shows Zeus, king of the Olympians, looking fierce and majestic.

Gifts were regularly offered to gods. A common gift-offering was a statue, often with a dedication on the base. All kinds of objects were offered: shields, vases, musical instruments, seals, rings and other items. On the Acropolis in Athens, there was a wash-basin, with the dedication: 'Smiythe the washer-woman dedicated this'.

Sanctuaries and Temples

The Greeks set aside spaces of land for their gods, called sanctuaries. A sanctuary could be anywhere: an open space, a rocky headland, a secluded valley or a spring. It was usually marked off by a line of stones, or a wall. Enclosed like this, it was called a *tenemos*. Inside would be the altar which could be a rock, a heap of stones, or even the growing mound of ash and bone that accumulated from sacrifices. Usually, altars were built of stone or brick, and whitewashed.

By the eighth century BC, temples began to be built in sanctuaries, as a kind of house for the god. There was usually a simple image of the god inside. The first temples were mud brick and wood. Then, from the seventh century BC, stone was used. People began to build great temples, whose ruins we can still see today.

▼ At the Delphic oracle, Apollo was thought to speak through a priestess, called the *Pythia*. Before giving her oracles, the *Pythia* had to bathe in holy water, drink from a holy spring and inhale the smoke from burning laurel leaves. She wore white, and held laurel leaves in her hand as she relayed the message from the god Apollo.

This inscription from 306 BC shows how one priest was employed by the local community:

'Gods! This sanctuary is rented to Diagnetos, son of Arkesilos from Melite, for ten years, for 200 drachmae each year. He must manage the sanctuary and the buildings, and whitewash the walls when necessary...'

He also had to tend the trees, open the shrine for the festival and lay out couches.

Oracles

An oracle was the response given by a god, when worshippers went to ask them questions about their future. Greeks never made decisions, such as whether to go to war or not, or where to start a new community, without consulting an oracle. The oracle would be interpreted by a priest or priestess, who would then repeat it to the worshipper. The most famous Greek oracle was the oracle of the god Apollo at Delphi.

People came from all over Greece and beyond to seek its advice. When Athens asked the Delphic oracle what to do about the conflict with the Persians, it was told to put its trust in 'wooden walls'. There was a great debate in the city as to what this meant. Themistocles argued that it meant ships, so the Athenians manned their ships, ready for war. Persia was defeated.

▶ Often the offerings to gods related to the service that the person wanted, or had gratefully received. The votive offering of a model of a leg suggests that somebody asked for their leg to be healed, and in thanks they have offered the god a symbol of that leg.

Rituals

The Greeks worshipped their gods through rituals – actions performed regularly. Prayer, for instance, is a ritual. The Greeks prayed often. They prayed to the gods by stretching their arms to the sky, and to the dead by hammering their fists on the ground. A *paean* was a great group shout or song of prayer.

Along with prayer, their most important ritual was sacrifice, which was seen as a gift offering to the gods. Animals were sometimes slaughtered and offered to a god. Different birds and animals had to be sacrificed to please different gods. There were special priests for each god, and if rituals were not followed exactly, it was believed that the gods would get upset. It was believed that the gods enjoyed the scent of the burnt flesh rising up to Mount Olympus. People also 'sacrificed' a portion of the things they produced or grew: corn, bread, cake, figs, olives or wool. Some of these might be burnt too.

Another common ritual which, like all Greek rituals, occurs frequently in Homer's stories, was libation. This involved the first part of a drink being poured onto the ground. Any important occasion needed a libation. When Greek cities made treaties with each other, they poured libations to seal the agreement. The Greek name for this, *spondai*, is also the word for treaty. Special libations were poured for the dead. A bowl of water was emptied onto a burial mound. The dead were called *dipsoi*, meaning 'the thirsty ones'.

▶ This vase shows women making offerings at a shrine. Greek families would pray at an altar in the courtyard of their houses. They would probably pray every day, to the relevant gods or goddesses. If they were about to harvest a crop, they would be praying to Demeter the goddess of fertility. But if they were going on a long journey, they might ask Hermes for good fortune on their travels.

Prayers were often written as poems. Some of them were not very serious, like this poem to Hermes god of thieves, written by Hipponax in about 540 BC :

'Please Hermes, I'm praying to you
because I'm shivering and frozen.
Get me, Hipponax, a nice woollen overcoat,
And a Persian cape and some felt slippers.
My teeth are rattling in my head.'

Festivals

Every *polis* usually had its own coins and its own calendar. It also had its own public religious festivals. Its public holy days were its public holidays – the only time off work that some Greeks had; they had no weekends. And the meat distributed after the sacrifices was often the only meat that many Greeks ate. Festivals were held to please the gods, so that they would grant good luck to the people of the *polis*.

A procession usually started the festival; groups of men and women carried food to sacrifice to the gods: cakes, honey, water and barley-meal. They would be singing hymns and dancing as they travelled. Athens had several festivals. The Great Panathenaea, held very four years in Athens, was the most famous of them. It consisted of processions, festivals and games, and lasted for six days. This festival celebrated the birth of Athene (who was the goddess of the Athenians). There was a war-dance, with performers imitating Athene being born out of the head of Zeus.

◀ A section of the frieze at the Parthenon shows the Panathenaea festival. The people in the procession are carrying a new embroidered robe, a *peplos*, to Athene. It was carried to the lower slopes of the Acropolis on a ship-cart, then taken to Athene's statue in the Erectheum (a small temple particularly sacred to the goddess).

Another way of discovering what would happen in the future, was by reading omens. This was usually done by someone who could see into the future, a 'soothsayer'. Omens might be seen in unusually coloured animals, birds screeching or blemishes on the entrails of sacrificed animals. During festivals, people took great care to protect themselves from seeing or hearing bad omens. They would cover their heads or have loud music played so that they could not hear. It was also regarded as very important to hear good omens. People would often call out the names of people who were well-respected or regarded as particularly lucky, to bring some of that luck to them.

◀ The Olympic Games were a religious event. Sacrifices took place on the first day, when priests attended. Winning was a way of offering the ultimate in human skills to Zeus. In their home cities, statues were erected to the winners. On their return they were paraded through the streets and poems in their praise were sung in public places. In Athens, victors were also given a large sum of money. The picture shows Olympia, the site of the Olympic Games.

CHAPTER 8

Art, Architecture and Literature

From the seventh century BC, Greeks were coming across many different cultures as they travelled around and set up new communities. Whereas before, design styles such as the Geometric style were abstract, repeated patterns, now artists were improving on this by trying to represent and glorify the human form. Greek art became very interested in the human body. Even now we use the Greeks' human terms for parts of vases: lip, neck, shoulder, foot and ears.

Sculpture

Sculptures were used to decorate temples and rich peoples' homes. They were also erected as signs of respect for the dead. In the Archaic Period (800–480 BC), most statues had fairly similar poses: formal and stiff, with arms by their sides and an unemotional facial expression.

◀ In 1972, a diver in the south of Italy, near Riace, saw legs sticking up out of the sand. Two bronze figures were eventually found – the Riace bronzes. From the sixth century BC statues were mainly being made from bronze. Because bronze was a valuable metal it was often melted down and reworked; so not many large bronzes exist today. This bronze shows Menelaus the brother of King Agamemnon.

The beautiful bronze sculpture of Poseidon throwing his trident, found in the sea off Cape Artemisium, could easily be any modern-day athlete hurling his javelin. Monuments built to honour the gods are full of human figures.

▼ Some pots were made from a type of clay that turned red when it was fired. The details were painted in a black paint which was made from clay and wood ash. This was called 'red-figure pottery'.

In the Classical Period (480–323 BC), Greek sculptors celebrated the gods and heroes with more skill. Facial expressions became detailed, and figures were shown in action. In the Hellenistic Period (281-31 BC), Greek art showed human emotions and the human body with much more skill. This was made possible by the greater understanding of anatomy and the nature of man. Whereas Classical sculpture had preferred to show beautiful young people, now sculptors portrayed old, wrinkled people. They showed all the human emotions, even the ugly ones.

Pottery

In the Archaic Period, scenes from mythology and everyday life began to appear on pots. The figures were more realistic than they had been before and they often showed oriental patterns, such as lotus flowers. This indicates that travel was allowing Greeks more contact with other cultures. Then in 550 BC, red pots decorated with black figures became very popular. This was called 'black-figure' pottery. Later, in the Hellenistic Period, moulded decorations on pots became more popular.

Architecture

After the fabulous architecture of the Mycenaean civilization, architecture in Greece became fairly simple in its shapes and materials, but looked very grand. Greek houses were usually mud and brick buildings with little detail in them, so architecture was mainly focused around the temple. It was here that architects could create their most fantastic pieces of work. Many architects of the time were also sculptors.

Two of the main styles of architecture in Greece were Doric and Ionic. Doric was a fairly solid, simple structure which was probably influenced by Mycenaean or Egyptian architecture. The columns of the Doric order were sturdy, with plain tops (capitals). Doric style was popular on mainland Greece. The Ionic order was a lighter and more elegant style with ornate details. Ionic columns were thinner, with a swirl at both sides of the top of the capital. These two styles were successfully combined by the architects of the Parthenon. Later, a more elaborate column, the Corinthian column, was also used.

▲ Built to honour the goddess of the city, Athene, between 447 and 438 BC, the Parthenon was constructed from 22,000 tonnes of the finest marble. The marble had iron in it, giving the structure a golden glow. The proportions of the building were modified to give the illusion of lightness, and the beautiful carvings and sculptures in the Parthenon were among the very best of classical Greek art.

Theatre and Drama

Below the Acropolis in Athens is a great theatre, built to seat perhaps 30,000 people. They sat on stone benches in the open air. The spectator could see and hear clearly from every seat. Such theatres, built in natural hollows, exist all through the Greek world. They are still used for festivals of Greek theatre. Just as the theatres have survived the centuries, so have the plays. Many Greek plays are still put on in theatres around the world every year.

▼ The theatre at Epidauros looks as though it had no seats, other than the step-like seating around the theatre. However, there were special carved stone seats at the front. Important people, such as priests and guests of honour, sat on these seats.

The first plays were mostly versions of the great Greek stories. In The Persians, *Aeschylus wrote about the Persian wars. He had fought at the battle of Marathon in 490 BC, and this vivid description of fighting at Salamis in 480 BC might suggest that he fought there too. A messenger is telling the Persian Queen Mother about the disaster:*

> *'At first the torrent of the Persian fleet bore up; but when the press of shipping jammed there in the narrows, none could help another, but our ships rammed each other, fouled each other and broke each others' oars.*
> *But those Greek ships... kept ringing round us and striking in, till ships turned turtle, and you could not see the water for blood and wreckage...'*

Drama was important, it was a part of every Athenians' education. During drama festivals the law-courts were closed and the Assembly did not meet. Admission was free to those who could not afford to pay. Many writers think women attended too.

These masks are reconstructions of the masks that actors wore in Greek theatre. The actors wore masks of linen and plaster. They were painted so that they would be easily visible from the back of the theatre. The expression on the mask showed whether the character was happy or sad, old or young, and what sex it was. Since no women acted in Greek plays, men needed masks to play a female part.

Greek drama first appeared as a countryside festival. Then the tyrant Peisistratus introduced the Dionysia festival in Athens, in honour of the god Dionysus. It lasted for five days; after the first day of processions and sacrifices, the remaining days were dramatic competitions. There were two types of plays performed – tragedies and comedies. One of the most famous tragic writers was Aeschylus, who was the first person to use more than one actor; he is regarded as the founder of Greek tragedy. Two other famous writers were Euripides, who often criticized governments and regimes in his plays, and Sophocles, who concentrated on human problems.

The Lenaea was a comedy festival. It took place early in the year. Comedies were usually about the politics and famous people of the day. They were very slapstick and often contained bawdy and rude jokes.

Poetry and Song

Poetry was considered a very important part of a boy's education in Greece. It was usually performed in public, often accompanied by music. The very first written-down Greek literature consisted of epigrams, very short poems, sometimes written as inscriptions. Compositions that had simply been remembered, were now written down. Hymns to the gods must have been sung from memory before writing arrived, but from the eighth century BC they were written. The poetess Sappho ran a school for girls, where they learnt to sing and write poems. These were regarded as important things for a young woman to learn. Sappho was thought to be one of the best Greek poets in the sixth century BC.

Plays and poetry recitals were often accompanied by music. There were also special songs for events such as births, deaths and religious festivals. One instrument played to accompany these songs was the *Kithara*, a lyre which was plucked at. Another was the *auloi*, a set of double pipes. According to Greek legend, the lyre had been invented by the god Hermes, who had constructed the instrument from a tortoiseshell and two ox horns.

▲ Aristophanes was the best-known comic writer in Greece. This scene from *Lysistrata*, one of his plays, has been painted onto a vase. In this play Aristophanes criticized the wars with Sparta. The story tells how the women of Athens decide they have had enough of war and go on strike, demanding an end to the conflict.

This is part of one of Sappho's surviving poems :
'Hesperus, herdsman of evening,
bringing back home
whatever the light of dawn
scattered: sheep
and goats to the fold,
children to mothers.'

CHAPTER 9

Science, Philosophy and Technology

Early Philosophers

Early Greeks used stories about the gods to answer questions about how the world worked and what man's purpose in life was. From the sixth century BC, some Greek thinkers began the search for practical solutions to these questions. In 585 BC, Thales accurately predicted an eclipse of the sun. He is also supposed to have measured the height of a pyramid by measuring the length of its shadow at exactly midday. In the 250 years or so after Thales, Greek thinkers invented a lot of ideas that have become familiar to us. These men were called philosophers, meaning 'lovers of knowledge'. Greek philosophers studied many subjects such as astronomy, biology, mathematics and geography.

The Sciences

Astronomy took a huge leap forward in about 270 BC, when Aristarchus announced that the earth moved on its axis around the sun. Although the idea is generally accepted now, at the time it was looked upon with scorn.

Anaxagoras, another important astronomer, realized that the light of the moon was produced by the reflection of the sun's light.

Plato wrote a dialogue, called **Meno.** *In it he shows Socrates the philosopher proving that a slave boy already understood a difficult geometric problem. Before he starts, he says to his listeners, 'Now kindly see whether he seems to be learning from me, or recollecting something.' In the end they agree that Socrates hadn't actually given him any information or knowledge. He hadn't 'taught' him anything, he had only asked questions to get to the answer.*

Mathematics was studied by great minds such as Archimedes and Pythagoras. Archimedes studied levers and pulleys, to work out how to use them to lift huge weights. He was a brilliant mathematician. Pythagoras' theory on triangles is still applied in classrooms all over the world. It is used to work out the length of the longest side of a triangle.

▲ Many Greek doctors believed that illnesses were carried in the blood. They therefore removed some of the patient's blood, to relieve the symptoms. If the wound became infected, this could be very dangerous. The patient might even die. This relief sculpture shows two bleeding cups and an open case of surgical instruments.

Medicine

Generally when people were ill they went to temples, made sacrifices to the gods and performed purification ceremonies. Many people believed that illness was a punishment from the gods. Hippocrates, a doctor who lived in the second half of the fifth century BC, was revolutionary in trying to understand what caused epilepsy. He also researched into other ailments, to try and find practical reasons for them. He founded a medical school. With his followers, he wrote many medical books discussing the use of practical cures, rather than the old fashioned religious ones.

◀ When people were ill, they often visited one of the temples of Asclepius. Asclepius was the son of Apollo. He had amazing healing powers and it was thought that if you slept one night in one of his temples your ailments would disappear. This photograph shows the remains of the therapy building and patient beds in the Asclepeion, in Pergamum, in Turkey.

Socrates and Plato

The Greek philosophers were concerned with finding out the best way for people to be living. The most famous Greek philosopher Socrates wrote nothing. He always said he knew nothing. Socrates challenged people to think about good and evil. He taught that nothing should be believed until it had been proved to be true. He taught using questions; we know this because a pupil of his, Plato, wrote down a lot of the things that Socrates had said. Plato wrote down conversations, or *dialogues*, in which Socrates and his friends discussed philosophical questions. Plato also wrote his own very famous works.

Aristotle and Science

Aristotle set up his own school, the Lyceum, in Athens, in about 335 BC. His 'writings' are probably lectures and notes collected into books by an editor. They show us how he invented the collecting and classifying techniques that we still use in science. Now, he might be called a biologist or zoologist. He also wrote and taught on physics, poetry and drama, ethics, colours, living things and politics. Even with politics, his method was to collect; he once said 'From collections of constitutions we examine what sort of thing preserves and what destroys cities.' Aristotle believed that knowledge only came from experience.

Travel Writing and Historians

One of the most famous Greek historians was Herodotus. He travelled thousands of miles on foot, on donkey, by camel and boat, to collect stories. He described the information that he collected as 'the traditions of various nations'. He said 'My underlying

▲ A bust of Plato. In about 385 BC Plato founded a school of philosophy in Athens. It was called the Academy. Plato wrote down his ideas on how to run an ideal state in his books, *The Republic* and *The Laws*. These books are still regarded as very important philosophical works. One of Plato's famous pupils was a young man from Macedonia in the north of Greece – his name was Aristotle.

principle is that it is what people have said to me, and what I have heard, that I must write down.'
Herodotus' main story is the history of the struggle between Persians and Greeks. He was interested in the effect that the Persian wars had on the ordinary people of ancient Greece.

Some of Herodotus' stranger travel stories have been proved to be true. He describes the amazing burials of the kings of the Scythians. Herodotus wrote that they buried a great chief, with his wagon and horses, sacrificed slaves, weapons, gold and other possessions. What Herodotus seems to have seen is exactly the kind of cart burial that has been found by archaeologists in the lands of the Celts.

▼ Socrates' philosophy, of knowledge through questioning, brought him to an early death. With his pupils, he spent a lot of time questioning the government and pointing out its faults. In the end his unpopularity caused him to be tried for corrupting the young. He was found guilty and sentenced to death by drinking poison. This fresco from Turkey, shows Socrates teaching.

History
Another early Greek historian was Thucydides. He was an Athenian who wrote a chronicle of the war between Athens and Sparta; he was a soldier in the war too. He died before he had finished the project. He describes battles and military expeditions, as well as the political quarrels of Athens. One of his methods of writing was to show his historical characters making speeches.

The two types of historical writing created by Herodotus and Thucydides influenced many later scholars. Xenophon of Athens, a pupil of Socrates, continued Thucydide's history up to 362 BC. Historians, during the reign of Alexander the Great, imitated Herodotus with their tales of exotic lands and strange peoples.

CHAPTER 10

The Hellenistic Age

After the Peloponnesian wars, both Athens and Sparta were more vulnerable to enemies. Sparta, especially, was growing weaker through a drop in the number of elite Spartan soldiers. Athens, although shaken by the wars with Sparta, began to recover wealth and confidence. In the fourth century BC, it gradually became a lively city again. But it was never able to dominate the region as it had done in the fifth century BC.

Athens and Sparta had been the two Greek states which at different times led others. They had even fought together against the Persians. But they had never managed, singly or together, to pull the world of the many Greek states together into one political unit, and ancient Greece never became an empire.

After the war

In 386 BC Sparta gave back the Ionian coastal cities to Persia. The result was another 'Athenian League' aimed at keeping Sparta under control. Occasional fighting broke out. Then Sparta and Thebes went to war. Thebes was trying to build an empire and it was becoming a threat. At Leuctra in 371 BC, Sparta was beaten by the Thebans. Ten years later, Sparta fought with Athens and other states against Thebes. Thebes won again. To add to the confusion, the Persians were threatening the Ionian states again. Then, in 359 BC, Philip ll became king of Macedon.

▼ It was rumoured that Philip's assassination had been planned by his power-hungry son Alexander. It was also possible that one of his rejected wives had paid for him to be murdered. When Philip's tomb was discovered, the skull was put back together and found to have a hole by the right eye. Philip had been hit by an arrow and lost his right eye; this was proof that it was Philip in the tomb.

Philip II of Macedon

Philip II of Macedon was king of a state that many Greeks gave little thought to; in their view it was hardly Greek at all, and nearly 'barbarous'. But in the 20 years after 359 BC, Philip made Macedon an extremely powerful state. With his professional army he took city after city into his control. By 342 BC Philip controlled the whole of Thrace, Thessaly and Chalkidike. That same year, the more nervous Greek states formed the Hellenic League against Philip. In 338 BC he marched his well-trained, experienced army into Boeotia. The Greeks faced him in battle two days later, and were defeated. Philip had gained control of Greece and as a result it was a united country. In 337 BC Philip announced a war against Persia. Now the Greek Macedonian Empire had a common cause; a common enemy.

Greece became part of the empire of the Macedonian kings; first Philip, then Alexander, his son. After his father's assassination, Alexander travelled a further 32,180 kilometres, conquering Persia, Pakistan and India, and eventually becoming known as Alexander the Great.

Aristotle the Greek philosopher, had been to the court of Philip, as tutor to Alexander, in 343–2 BC. In his writings he advised Alexander to be, 'a leader to the Greeks and a despot to the barbarians. To look after the Greeks as friends and relatives, and to do as you want with the barbarians, treating them as you would animals or plants.'

◀ Alexander's cavalry were famous for their successes. Noblemen usually joined the Companion Cavalry, an elite military group which was originally part of the king's bodyguard. They wore a cuirass with boots and a helmet, and carried very long spears. Their task was to break up the enemy infantry's formation.

Alexander the Great

Alexander conquered huge areas in Asia minor, Afghanistan, Iraq, Iran, India and Egypt. He founded many new Greek cities, such as Alexandria in Egypt. These cities were Greek, with Greek constitutions, and Greek citizens. Alexander replaced some governors of conquered cities with his own men. Wherever he conquered he left Greeks behind, ensuring that the Greek language and culture spread across a huge area. At the battle of Issus in 333 BC, Alexander defeated the Persians. In this new empire he included Persians in the government; he had realised that his empire was now too big to be run successfully from Greece. In 323 BC Alexander died of a fever. No plans had been made for the future of the empire, and it was divided up and fought over by some of Alexander's generals.

▲ Alexander the Great founded many new cities, most of which he named Alexandria, after himself.

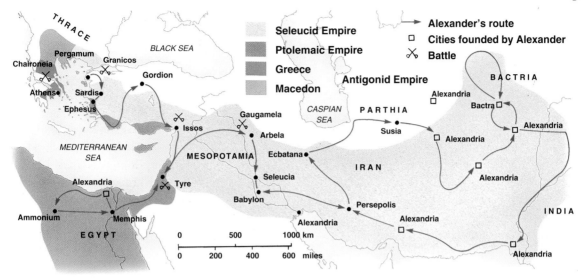

▲ This map shows the route that Alexander and his army took on their military campaigns. It is also divided into the three main empires that were formed on the death of Alexander.

The Hellenistic Age

Even though Alexander was dead, Greek culture and ideas still dominated the empire. The cities of the Hellenistic world were spread far and wide, but no matter where they were, they were basically Greek. Their art, language, law and architecture were influenced by Greece; even in cities as far away as Syria. This time, from 336–322 BC, was called the Hellenistic Age, from the Greek word *Hellene*, which means 'Greek'. Power struggles in the empire had resulted in it collapsing, until the Battle of Ipsus in 301 BC. After this battle, four kingdoms were set up. They were all ruled by kings, called *Diadochi*. After more fighting, three large kingdoms were established. They were ruled by Ptolemy, Seleucus and Antigonas. The Antigonid family dominated Greece, but some Greek states allied with the Romans who had conquered most of Italy and Sicily by 200 BC.

The largest city in the world by 200 BC was Alexandria in Egypt. It had a great library, with perhaps half a million manuscripts. Thousands of works of Greek literature, science and philosophy were kept there. It gradually became a centre of learning and commerce, and its famous port was one of the busiest in the world. The great marble lighthouse, the Pharos which stood at the port, was one of the seven wonders of the world.

King Philip of Macedon helped Hannibal, the Carthaginian general, to fight against Rome. But, in 168 BC the Romans defeated the Macedonians at the battle of Pydna. Then, in 146 BC, they made Macedon and Greece provinces of the Roman Empire. The Seleucid family took longer to come under Roman rule. The constant rebellions and wars in their many provinces weakened their empire. Finally, in 64 BC the Roman general Pompey seized their lands. The Ptolemies ruled quite a stable empire. They had kept their Greek culture and introduced many Greek ways of life to Egypt, where they governed. Eventually, in 31 BC the Romans defeated Queen Cleopatra of Egypt and her Roman ally, Mark Antony, at the Battle of Actium. The last Hellenistic kingdom was finally under Roman rule.

▼ The Roman emperor Hadrian loved Athens and lived there for several years. He commissioned a lot of building in Roman Athens. The mixture of Roman and Greek architectural styles is visible in buildings that we still see today. Around AD 130, he finished the Temple of Olympian Zeus in Athens, which had been started by Peisistratus. This picture shows Hadrian's Arch, built in Athens in the second century BC.

Greece and Rome

A Roman poet, Horace, summed up the effect of the Greeks on the Romans 'Greece, though conquered, conquered its wild conqueror.' The Romans were very impressed by Greek achievements, and as Greece was sucked into the Roman Empire, it became obvious that the Romans were willing to learn from the Greeks. Educated Romans spoke fluent Greek. Their religion borrowed the Greeks' gods, their sculptors echoed Greek figures and artists, and writers and builders used Greek ideas for inspiration. The Romans helped to keep Greek culture alive by studying and enjoying it, just as we still do today.

Timeline

All dates are BC

THE BRONZE AGE
c. 2000 Arrival of first Greek-speaking peoples on mainland Greece.
c. 2000–1750 First Minoan palaces are built. Rise of Minoan culture on Crete.
c. 1700 Destruction of first Minoan palaces, possibly by earthquake.
c. 1600 Rise of Mycenaean culture in Greece.
c. 1200 Traditional date of the start of the Trojan war. Many Mycenaean palaces abandoned.

THE DARK AGE
1100 Mycenaean culture disappeared.
900 Sparta is founded.

THE ARCHAIC PERIOD
c. 800 Greeks adapt Phoenician writing to create their own language.
776 First Olympic Games.

c. 750 Homer believed to have been alive.
c. 750 Founding of colonies in areas of the Mediterranean and Black Sea as Greeks emigrate from mainland Greece.
c. 594 Solon made archon of Athens, new laws to protect the poor.
585 Thales of Miletus predicts eclipse of sun.
545 Conquest of Ionian Greeks by the Persians.
534 The first Greek tragedy was performed.
c. 508 Kleisthenes reforms political system in Athens.

THE CLASSICAL AGE
500–449 Wars against the Persians.
490 Persians invade Greek mainland and are beaten at the Battle of Marathon.
480 Battle of Salamis and Battle of Thermopylae.
478 Beginning of the Delian league, leading to the growth of the Athenian empire under Pericles.
447–432 The Parthenon was built.
431–404 Peloponnesian war between Athens and Sparta.
430 Plague in Athens.
404 Sparta defeats Athens.

399 Socrates put to death.
359 Philip II becomes King of Macedon.
338 Conquest of Greece by Philip of Macedon.
336–323 Reign of Alexander the Great.

THE HELLENISTIC PERIOD
281 Three *diadochi* kingdoms set up.
215–205 Macedonians and Romans go to war.
202–197 Second Macedonian war.
171–168 Third Macedonian War.
146 Romans destroy Corinth.
64 Romans conquer remains of Seleucid kingdom.
31 Battle of Actium. Defeat of the last Hellenistic ruler.

Glossary

Acropolis Meaning 'high city' in Greek, the Acropolis was the city fortress built on a hill for security.

Agora A gathering place, a city square.

Archaic Period 800–500 BC, the time after the Dark Age when Greek civilization began to prosper.

Archon An Athenian government official.

Aristocrat Meaning 'best people' aristocrats were rich landowners.

Attica Athens and the surrounding area.

Bronze Age 3000–1100BC, the period when bronze was used for making tools and weapons.

Capital The top of an architectural column which was often elaborately decorated.

Chiton A dress worn by Greek women.

Citizen A free man who was part of a city state.

Classical Age 500–336 BC, the period after the Archaic Period and before the Hellenistic Age, when Athens went to war with Persia and then Sparta. The famous statesman Pericles was leader of Athens during the Classical Age.

Cuirass Armour breastplate worn by Greek cavalry.

Dark Age 1100–800 BC, the period after the breakdown of Mycenaean civilization. The art of writing was lost, so historians have very little information on this time.

Democracy Government by the body of citizens, when all citizens have a say in the government of their state.

Demos The people of a state.

Diadochi The 'successors' or generals who split Alexander the Great's empire between them when he died.

Doric order A style of architecture which used plain columns and capitals.

Ecclesia The assembly of Athenian citizens that debated proposals put to it by the council, the *Boule*.

Fresco A wall painting made by painting directly onto wet plaster.

Golden Age 479–431 BC, a period in Athens' history, after the Persian wars, when Athens became a cultural and financial centre for Greece.

Gymnasium A centre for sporting activities which later developed into a hall of intellectual discussion and learning.

Hellenistic Age The period after the death of Alexander the Great, when Greek culture was prominent across his former empire and the Greek language flourished.

Hetairai Women who were educated and trained to entertain men at dinner parties.

Himation A cloak worn by Greek men and women.

Hoplite A heavily armed Greek foot soldier.

Ionians The Greek cities and settlements on the coast of Asia Minor (now called Turkey).

Ionic order A style of architecture which used slender columns with curling tops or capitals.

Libation When the first part of a drink was poured onto the ground as an religious offering to the gods.

Linear A Minoan form of writing, undeciphered.

Linear B Mycenaean writing adapted from the Minoan Linear A.

Long walls Walls that ran from Athens to its port at Piraeus.

Metic The name given at Athens to foreigners resident in Attica.

Minoan The civilization that lived on Crete from 2000–1450 BC.

Mycenaean The civilization that dominated Greece from 1600–1100 BC.

Oligarchy Government by a few.

Omen A sign from the gods, such as a bird falling from the skies, warning of something that will happen in the future.

Oracles Prophecies, given by a god or goddess, interpreted by a priest or priestess.

Ostracism The ritual of voting to send people into exile, by scratching their names on o*straca*, bits of broken pottery.

Paidogogus A slave who had the duty of looking after his master's son. He had to teach the boy how to behave and attend to his needs whenever he went out to school or to the *gymnasium*.

Phalanx Greek order of battle where heavy infantry moved forward in an unbroken line, several ranks deep.

Philosophy Originally, 'the love of wisdom', or study of all areas of the worlds. Later it became more specific and related to trying to gain an understanding of the purpose of life.

Polis The city state and its people.

Shaft graves Deep Mycenaean tombs.

Soothsayer A person who had been trained to read omens to see into the future.

Strategos An Athenian army commander. In the Athenian democracy there were ten strategoi elected every year. Their job was to put into effect the policies which had been voted in by the Assembly.

Trireme A ship with three banks of oars.

Tyranny Government by one person who had absolute control.

Further Reading

Ancient History Atlas by Michael Grant (Weidenfeld, 1971)

Ancient Greece by John Ellis Jones (Kingfisher, 1992)

A Greek Temple by Fiona Macdonald (Simon and Schuster, 1992)

Greeks by Rachel Wright (Watts, 1992)

Ancient Greeks by Anita Ganeri (Watts, 1993)

The Greeks by S. Peach and A. Millard (Usborne, 1990)

Index